Effective Strategies for Human Service Professionals in a Client-based Setting

By STEPHANIE WILLIAMS MHSSA

Build2Bridge, Inc.

Brookhaven, GA

www.build2bridge.com

Ordering Information:

Quantity sales. Special discounts are available on quantity purchases by corporations, associations, and other entities. For details, contact the publisher at the address above.

For orders by U.S. trade bookstores and wholesalers, please contact Build 2 Bridge, Inc. build2bridge@gmail.com

Printed in the United States of America

Our hope is that we remind you, help you, or challenge you to flourish by utilizing the tools demonstrated in this workbook.

The author has made every effort to ensure the accuracy of the information contained in this book was correct at time of publication. The author does not assume and hereby disclaims any liability to any party for any loss, damage, or disruption caused by errors or omissions, whether such errors or omissions result from accident, negligence, or any other cause.

Content

PREFACE

After 20 years of working in the Social Services field, I have met a wide variety of professionals. As a Human Service professional, I am a Veteran, worked in Higher Education and the mental health field. I have learned how to perform properly and (unfortunately) improperly throughout my career. The paradox here is the take-away value: the when, the how, and the why. I choose to share the strategies I have learned and are still learning that are often over looked. These strategies, when not followed, cost companies and society billions of dollars each year. Our actions effect every aspect of our careers and the lives of others.

Everyone will need to consider their own personal motives, skills, and natural talent. But you can achieve your desired results by working on yourself. Applying these simple but practical exercises to your everyday practice as a Human Service professional will set a tone in your office, with your teams, and for new employees.

You will see this statement throughout the workbook: ***"Think outside the box but stay within policy."***

We implore you to be creative and confident, but to do so with your company's policies always in mind.

The places you'll go depends on you.

The Human Service Professional & Case Management

Who are Human Service Professionals and what do they do? Human Service professional skills are vital in the community and within the facilities we service. As a Human Service professional, your platform may involve elderly care, education, criminal justice, public policy and so many other great fields. Your contributions impact lives by the service you provide daily.

As mentioned above, there are many types of careers that exemplify the importance of diversity in the field of your profession. Let's look at some of those roles more closely, such as, case management and the essential domains.

As a Human Service professional, case management becomes vital when ensuring proper customer service, ethical practice, and the assistance to help identify roadblocks between the client, provider and their treatment. It is best to understand that case management transcribed though annotation provides a better understanding or, if you will, an illustration of service of an individual's care. Case management is not a profession it is a cross-disciplinary and interdependent specialty practice. Case Mangers help identify appropriate providers and facilities throughout the range of services. They are ensuring that available resources are being used in a timely and cost-effective manner to obtain the finest value for both the client and the reimbursement source.

List the ways case management aids client-provider relations? are there other ways case management aids in client-provider relations?

This is exercise will help you *think outside the box* (but to stay within policy!).

List the ways case management aids client-provider relations?

Think Outside the Box

As a case manager, this is a very important role. As case managers, your documentation ensures a positive or negative outcome. You are a leader who demonstrates to others how to advocate for themselves to promote wellness. You are responsible for the accuracy of the accounts of treatment and service the individual receives as they progress.

Some roles include more hands-on service than others. Every role no matter the setting, is vital. Some settings require you to provide one-on-one care to individuals or groups. These settings need case managers. Your job may require you to work long hours, which may include weekends, holidays, and flex-shifts.

Maybe you are utilizing this workbook because you are new to the field of Human Service. This is your big opportunity to make an impact on a larger scale by working efficiently for a great organization such as

_________________________ (fill in your organization).

If you are a born leader, you can take an average organization and make it an exceptional one by doing what is fair and ethical, going above and beyond.

Remember this when it comes to documenting your case notes. Your case notes are your fingerprint. If you did not write it down, it did not happen.

This is exercise will help you *think outside the box* but stay within policy.

Will my case notes affect my organization
overall effectiveness?

How can I improve my case notes?

Useful Words List for Note Taking

Acknowledged

Actively Listened

Addressed

Advised

Advocated

Asked

Assisted

Challenging

Checked In

Clarified

Collaborated

Commended

Confronted

Conducted

Conveyed

Crisis Intervention

Developed

Educated

Empathized

Empowered

Encouraged

Ensured

Established

Explained

Explored

Expressed

Facilitated

Focusing/Refocusing

Framing/Reframing

Goal (setting)

Development/Goal Setting

Guided

Highlighted

Honoring

Identified

Information Giving/Gathering

Informed

Interacted

Interpreted

Joined

Modeled

Observed

Physical Activity

Played

Praised

Presented

Probed

Problem Solving

Prompted

Rapport-building

Recapped

Recommended

Redirected

Reflected

Reflective Listening

Reframed

Reinforced

Reiterated

Reminded

Reviewed

Role-played

Social Skills Practice

Suggested

Supported

Teaching/Lecturing

Urge

Effective Case notes begin with self-statements

✓ I agree to state the facts, be Non-judgmental, and utilize
neutral language when writing my case notes.

Are you ready to become an **Effective Human Service Professional?** If so, let's begin.

Communication

Have you ever met someone, and immediately you became uncomfortable? Have you ever asked yourself why this is? Most times it is based on the body language of others. If we are honest with ourselves, we know our body language can shift the environment. Did you realize that your body language can influence how people approach you, or communicate with you?

 Communication skills, such as listening, and your tone can generate respect. Body language, such as eye contact, etc., encourages empathy, feedback, and even clarity.

Ask yourself, how has my body language helped build rapport, communicate or deterred clients and co-workers?

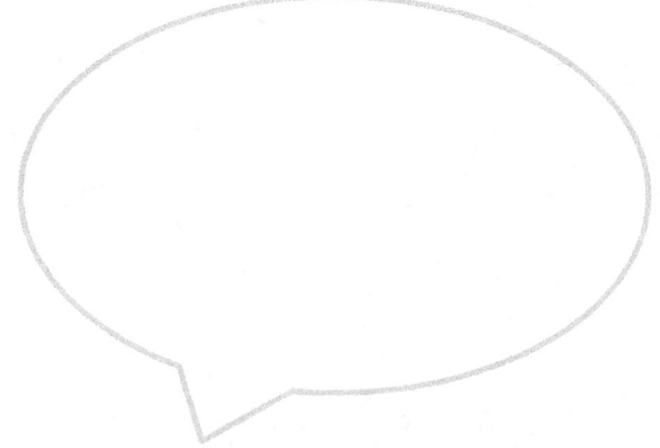

What are your *nonverbal* cues saying to others?

____
____
____
____
____
____
____
____
____
____
____
____
____
____
____
____

*Did you know, how **YOU** see things matter?*

Here are some tips on how to display positive body language:

Let's do the work!

1. Posture.

Posture reinforces your attitude about yourself and others.

2. Handshakes.

A firm handshake sends nonverbal communication cues that can set the entire mood of your conversation.

3. Slowing down your speech.

Breath. Focus. Stay calm. This will allow your audience to clearly understand each point you are trying to convey.

Do the Work.

Now, practice these positive body language exercises as a mirror exercises, either individually or in your groups.

What did you discover? How does your body language impact Others?

Tone

Now let's define tone.

____

____

____

____

____

Tone in whatever setting or subject matter communicates your feelings and ultimately affects others.

Ask yourself

How am I making others feel when I give feedback, greetings or instructions? Does it provoke bitterness, or edify others?

How does my communication affect others when I am tired, aggravated or cheerful?

Our tone will represent our true intention and may display aggravation, boredom, weariness, or gratefulness.

Pet Peeves

Things that make you irritated, also known as Pet
Peeves. In this section, list the pet peeves you have
IDENTIFIED that seem to block your communication
at times.

Pet Peeves.	The Reality.

Person A **Pet Peeve:** Others do not give me direct
eye contact. **The Reality**: shyness, culture, mental
health, disability.

Tone

Exercise 1.

Write down a time where your tone was opposite from your intentions.

____

____

____

____

____

____

____

____

____

____

How could you better communicate your statements
or replies?

____

____

____

____

____

How does your tone and your delivery impact
others?

____

____

____

____

____

____

____

____

____

Exercise 2.

Respect

Let's define respect.

____
____
____
____
____

Are there people in your life that you respect? If so, who are they?

____
____
____
____
____
____

What is your definition of respect? (Given or received?)

What does **respect** look like as it pertains to your clients, customer, and co-workers?

____

____

____

____

____

____

____

____

____

____

____

____

Just remember to keep pushing. This is only the beginning. You can get through this! This is helping you so you can help others.

Empathy

Define **empathy** in our own words. Discuss.

____

____

____

____

____

____

____

____

____

____

____

____

✔ **Empathy is the ability to understand the thoughts, feelings or emotions or someone else.**

List examples of empathy that you have experienced recently.

____

____

____

Discussion.

When are there times to practice empathy?

____
____
____
____
____
____
____
____
____
____

What does empathy mean to you?

____
____
____
____

Now that we have thoroughly worked on empathy, ask yourself, are your actions and the definition of **empathy** aligned with one another?

____
____
____
____
____
____
____
____
____

If so, are you practicing it as you daily interact with others?

____
____
____
____
____
____
____
____
____
____
____

The Magnificent 7

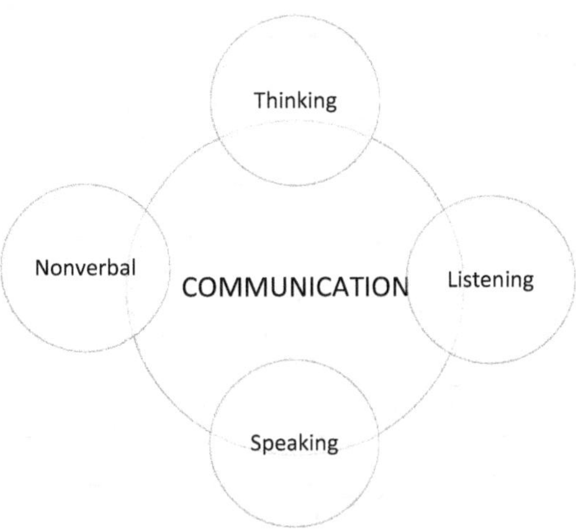

Effective communication skills will always include The Magnificent *7*

- ✓ Active listening
- ✓ Using appropriate nonverbal communication
- ✓ Using appropriate voice and tone
- ✓ Communication at the case-level of understanding
- ✓ Giving information
- ✓ Using reinforcement
- ✓ Summarizing important points from the conversation

Effective Note Taking

Breath

What does your communication style say to others? Let's investigate further.

📌 You have the absolute authority to make your body language your Super Power. The way you stand, position your body, and make eye contact are cues that speak to others. Your body language

determines how others approach you, even to the point of trusting you.

Negative Body Language	Positive Body Language

⏳ Now take some time and reflect, you deserve it!

TOOLS

knowl·edge

/ˈnäləj/

noun
1. 1.
    facts, information, and skills acquired by a person
    through experience or education; the theoretical or
    practical understanding of a subject.

Tools for Your Tool Belt

Are you mastering your tools? Just remember, when you present your tools to a client you are presenting your organization.

The tool belt is essential for clients as they rebuild their lives. They will find the road to recovery challenging. So, how you present these tools is important.

 **Your style and delivery matters**.

Here's an example of a tool that is useful for a residential setting.

- Knowledge and efficiency for medication management

List more tools below that are related to your position.

____

____

____

____

 Group setting and utilizing tools.

What approach do you find effective in a group setting?

Here are some examples of group setting tips.

1. CHOSE THE TOPICS wisely
2. SET UP YOUR ROOM
3. Present YOUR INFORMATION with an outline
4. MANAGE your time wisely
5. CLOSE YOUR GROUPS effectively

Depending on the goals of your facilitation style, remember that your setting depends on the number of participants. It is important. I always like to encourage others to use an inclusive environment, in which members feel respected by and connected to one another, if possible.

Keep discussions tasteful. Have fun but stay within ethical standards and policies because you are representing your organization.

Consider these **5** points with me. How can you exemplify effective communication?

- *Confrontation*

  ____
  ____
  ____
  ____

- *Active Listening*

  ____
  ____
  ____
  ____

- *Location*

  ____
  ____
  ____
  ____

- *Reframing*

  ____
  ____
  ____
  ____

- *Deferring*

  ____
  ____
  ____
  ____

Evaluating Effective Professionalism

Are effective business affair, meetings or conferences important to you? Use the space below to write down a time when you felt you did not practice effective professionalism to the best of your ability. This could have been early in your career. Ask yourself what have you learned?

____

____

____

____

____

____

____

____

____

____

____

____

Define **professionalism** in your own words.

____

____

____

____

____

____

____

Defined.

Professionalism is competency. Professionalism is the ability to do your work properly and to standard. By doing this means doing your best. This means always giving correct information.

Tools

Here are some tools for your toolbox:

- Speak clearly
- Be present
- Take notes and take detailed data to ensure you are well-informed.
- Know your audience
- Know your content
- Master your craft

NOTES:

Professional Goals:

____
____
____
____
____
____
____
____
____
____
____
____
____
____

If you are in a group or training, this is a great time to take a break.

Professionalism Principles

Are you asking yourself, "what are *Professionalism Principles?*

Personally, I like to think of Professionalism as the motivation to set healthy boundaries. I also think this section of the workbook will help to remind you, the Human Service professionals to effectively set healthy boundaries. Early in my career, I learned that setting healthy boundaries determined the effectiveness of change in the clients, students and peers I assisted. I set healthy boundaries and continue to study the in-depth nature of boundaries in the lives of those we serve as a Human Service professional and as it pertains to my own personal wellness.

It is my hope that as you begin to make decisions that are geared toward excellence, these *Professionalism Principles* will remind you, as they have reminded me, of the steps, mindsets, and wisdom you need to implement to do your job effectively.

Starting here.

Be Mindful.

 Should what you wear to an event, services provided meeting, or home visit matter? What are your views on presentation?

____

____

____

____

____

____

____

What does "professional" mean in the context of todays' business meetings and home visitation. A professional should consider presenting themselves neat in appearance for the office and meetings. They should exceed the requirements of their organizations dress code, taking the steps to prepare for a meeting or visit. The time of the meeting, the weather, and the location should be considered. These factors will determine if you are ready for the next level in your career management.

Project Confidence.

Effective confidence is the act of projecting confidence and not arrogance. Above all, being polite and well-spoken in any interaction with clients, vendors, management, and co-workers. This will allow room for great dialog. Remember to stay calm, even during tense situations.

____

____

____

____

____

____

____

____

____

____

____

____

____

____

Be Trustworthy.

Being a trustworthy person doesn't just happen. It takes commitment, dedication, and a choice to live an honest life.
What are your beliefs about a trustworthy person?

____

____

Now let's discuss these **9** Trustworthy Traits!

Keep your commitment in word and deed

Be honest

Be transparent

Be on time

Keep confidences

Don't gossip

Apologize

Be predictable

Set the tone

Let's do the work and discuss this further. (20 min)

Display Competency

Can we all agree that leadership in turbulent times are more effective when leaders prepare. Leadership is more than managing communication.

Containing a crisis has a long-term effect on the organization. The blame can impact the organization and make it hard to recover. So, the display of competency is vital in a crisis.

Define Crisis

____

____

A crisis is either an unexpected or a smoldering problem. An unexpected crisis is one that you did not see coming. A client having an episode, or an employee damaging property could be a crisis.

A crisis can be *anything*. A smoldering crisis is one that is perceived as the responsibility and fault of the organizational leader. This means you.

List smoldering crisis.

1.

2.

3.

4.

5.

6.

What are the phases of a crisis? Signal detection, Preparation, Containment, Business Recovery, and Learning.

Phases of a Crisis

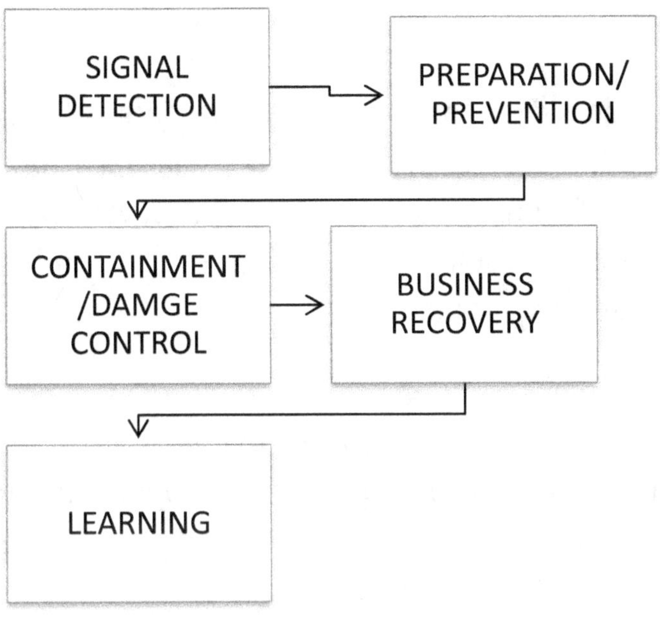

What We Know

Signal detection prompts us to ask the question, what situations and practices does the organization ignore that may lead to a crisis? While preparation and prevention are important, you should ask, Has the organization's culture developed a readiness mentality for responding to a crisis?

What are some of your organization's signal detections or preparations?

Ethical decision making is a process. When a conflict arises, this area can be hard for some. Don't be that someone. In general, ethics are the manner of helping in the time of need and addressing issues.

Be the person who strives to ensure resources are available. Ensure equality and opportunity for all persons. Be the professional that seeks to resolve conflict between clients' interests in a socially responsible manner that upholds the standards of ethics at all time. Ethical decision-making involves seeking to build relationships and bridging relationships among people that are purposeful.

Ethical decision-making is continuous. As a professional, it is your responsibility to practice truth. As a final note, ethical-decision making includes education. As a professional, your skills and knowledge are valuable, but only if you are willing to use the tools.

How are you practicing ethics daily?

Maintain Your Poise

Your most important asset in the workplace my not
be what you think.

It is important to always show a level of care with a
level of calm. Poise demonstrated under pressure
illustrates control. Poised people are well-mannered.
They are powerful because poise commands respect.

What is more comforting than mutual respect?
Consider the importance of great eye contact,
appropriate attire for the workplace, and confidence.

How in the past week have you maintain your poise
in a stressful situation?

____
____
____
____
____
____
____

Use Proper Etiquette.

If you are like most professionals, you have a mentor and have taken classes that shape your working relationships. But did you know how important office etiquette is?

An office is not a social gathering. Noise should always be kept to a minimum. Personal phone calls should be personal. At all costs, avoid taking calls at your desk while you are speaking with clients or colleagues. Cell phone ringtones and email alerts should be on silent. They are great distractions. In addition, it could cause you to miss out on important information.

Show up on time. Yes, some situations are unavoidable. However, do your best to show up. Showing up is a battel won, unless you are sick. If you are sick, then you should stay home.

We can all appreciate light scents or lavender or tulips. But one should save it for your time off with family and friends. Avoid wearing perfumes and colognes at work. Certain smells trigger migraines in some. Or they may trigger memories that may or may not be emotional. Just be mindful of others.

Keep It Brief When Sending Written Correspondence

When you start respecting time, you also respect the time of others. So, it is important to send brief emails with no errors. Errors cause communication confusion. It is important to remember the **9** Common Rules:

Introduce yourself. Relax. Mirror the other person. Respond. Respond promptly. Correct your grammar and capitalization. Write with warmth. And proofread, proofread, proofread!

Remember that the email is a conversation, whether you are responding or leading in the email. Yes, you should be relaxed. There are cases that you should be formal. However, "Dude what's good?" is too relaxed. Be sure to mirror your correspondent, following their lead. Make sure you sign off each email with your title and contact information. Keep it short. Some examples of a sign off that you should remember, including: Best, My Best, Best Regards, or Warm Regards.

List some of the sign offs you use today and have used in the past.

Sign Offs

Reminder

Emails should always have the following:

- Subject line describing why you're writing
- Greeting
- Short message (2-3 paragraphs at the most)
- Closing
- Signature with your contact information

This is great place to take a break. You have done a great job! Take time to jot down your thoughts.

NOTES:

THINK
POSITIVE

NOTES:

Optimistic

Show Compassion

NOTES:

Add your own affirmation or action word!

NOTES:

Add your own affirmation or action word!

Tools for your Tool Belt

Are you mastering your tools? Just remember, when you present your tools to a client, you are presenting your organization.

Your style and delivery matters.

Prioritize

Quiet the Noises in Your Head.

Remember Self-Care

Coping with Stressors

Transference and Counter-transference

Organizational Changes

Time Management

The Tool Belt are essential for your inventory of skills. Here are some refresher talking points to consider and exercise.

Prioritize

Feeling overwhelmed at work is normal, who are we kidding? Everyone has had this moment more times than most would like to admit.

I believe it is important to have an organized system that works best for you. It should work not just for you, but also for those working with you in case of an emergency. One motivation to encourage your organizing skills is to remember that you are part of a team. When you are overwhelmed is a perfect time to ask for help. Now, your coworkers will be working, and they will either be working in chaos or in order. But they will help you if they can. So, reach out—it can't hurt! It is critical to stay organized while mastering your skills.

Your ability to improve your organizational skills and prioritize tasks is a measure of your overall competence.

The best advice to follow is to create a To-Do list, which should have a master list, a monthly list weekly list, and a daily list. You will have time to practice this toward the end of the workbook. But I hope you are already doing this.

Did you know?

The 80/20 Rule

20% of your efforts tends to produce 80% of your results. So, prioritizing is a must.

PRIORITES

```
E A L D T O T X Z R X H N L K
I C N I D R F C G X I G A I S
G H F O S M A J R Y Z N A W A
H I T O C T O M C G O J Q R T
T E R E S P O N S I B L I T Y
Y V T I M E E K T T V N V K S
T E S Y W C I A Y H V B Z D W
W X U D I L Z Q F E L M T E X
E E F F L I T V S D Q Y C T E
N E F S N L U T W A B S X A M
T E J A G E M Y L K E E W V J
Y Z G T N E M E G A M A M I Q
S R Z P N E V A L U A T E T U
O M G T P P T O C Z O V U O Q
M M R V P B K N A V L O V M W
```

ACHIEVE
EFFICENCY
EIGHTYTWENTY
EVALUATE
INVESTMENT
LIST
MAMAGEMENT
MONTHLY
MOTIVATED
ORGANIZATIONAL
RESPONSIBLITY
SKILLS
SMART
TASK
TIME
TODO
WEEKLY

Quiet the Noises in Your Head.

With all the social media post, apps, and wellness programs out there, no one should have problems using the tools provided to quit the noises in our heads.

The issue is not the tools but the overwhelming number of tools. What did we do before phone apps and social media? Well, we took walks, we sat on our porches and watched the trees. We listened to the birds. Even if you lived in the city, there was a moment of quietness because you found it within.

The stress is real, and finding internal quietness is important. Take a breath or two away from your routine. Eat lunch alone, tasting your food and feeling the coolness or warmth of your tea or signature coffee. Utilize the five senses. This can quiet the mind. Think about the last meal you enjoyed. What did it taste like? Do you remember the smell of the vegetables and the sweetness of the dessert? That is called being present. When you are present, your mind is quite because you have now stopped stressing and the clutter seems to disappear.

In Human Service, especially in a residential setting, having a decluttered mind can make an enormous difference in how you manage clients' safety.

Self-Care

Self-care starts with you. When we starve our purpose by suppressing our creativity or ignoring the relationships around us, we neglect the best things that we have going: **SELF**.

I came up with these words to help me remember how I should prioritize my self-care. What words can you come up with to help as you practice self-care?

S- submitting

E- empowering

L- living

F- freedom

S	E	L	F

Assessment

ASSESSMENT

Here is an assessment to gauge where you are. This is not set in stone, but it will give you some insight. Take your time as a group or individually and discuss it.

The scale is rated:

X – never happens
0 – I don't do this
1 – rarely happens
2 – occasionally happens
3 – frequently happens

Physical Self-care
_Eat healthy meals
_Get regular medical check ups
_Take time off when sick
_Enjoy friends and family
_Take vacations
_Get plenty of sleep

Mental Self-care
_ Explore your surroundings
_ Listen to your thoughts and feelings – and take inventory
_ Read books unrelated to work
_ Take small vacations
_ Write in a journal
_ Say no to extra responsibilities that would over-stress you

Emotional self-care

_ Have fun with friends and family
_ love yourself
_ Go to the movies - take yourself on dates
_ Identifying those things that make you happy brings you joy
_ Rehearse verbal affirmations
_ Other:

Spiritual self-care

_ Make time for the God of my understanding
_Pray
_Sing
_Meditate
_Contribute to a worthy cause in the community
_ Have an "Awe" moment
_Be open to not knowing

Relationship Self-care

_ Ask for help when I need it
_ Enlarge my friendship circle
_Stay connect to faraway friends and family
_Share my feelings with others
_Schedule regular dates with those you love and cherish

Workplace or Professional Self-Care

_ Take schedule breaks
_Advocate your needs
_ Have Peer Support
_ Set Boundaries
_ Arrange work space that fits your needs
_ Make time for silence

List some other Self Care habits you may wish to incorporate in your everyday life.

1.

2.

3.

4.

5.

Coping with Stressors

Depression in the workplace is real and should be taken seriously. The real question is what is happening on the job that is causing you stress? Years ago, I realized that work depression can have symptoms such as headaches, nausea, and even anxiety.

Identifying your stressor is the first step, but addressing it is the leap. One should act rather than react. The reaction given toward a stressor can cause more stress if not calculated properly. The importance of stepping back, taking inventory, and then taking a deep breath can ease a tense situation.

Here is what to consider addressing the stress at work and to feel better about yourself.

De-stress your body. Take 15-minutes and utilize your brake time. Go on walks. Stress can cause a chain reaction to our physical bodies. Even a short, brisk walk can be very beneficial.

- Eat well. Okay, I know sweets are tempting, but sugar could add to stress because sugar causes the body to crash. So, instead of a cinnamon bun, grab water, fruit, and green healthy food.

Who doesn't love a good nap? Have you considered taking a power nap? A good nap could clear up foggy-brain. If naps are not your thing, set a schedule to go to bed earlier. Leaving your phone in the kitchen and silencing the ring tone can assist in reducing the anxiety of being on the phone. Nothing beats stress like a good night's sleep.

NOTES:

Share below how you practice de-stressing.

> *Relax*
>
> *Refresh*
>
> *Recharge*

Extraordinary You

Transference and Countertransference

We consciously or unconsciously transfer emotional responses (either feelings or attitudes) from the past onto people and situations in the present. Let's dive in a little deeper.

Think of your significant other, or maybe a close acquaintance. Reflect on some part of their behavior that you have a strong response to, either positively or negatively. Now write that down on a piece of paper. Describe what that part of their personality is like, and how you react in your thoughts, feelings, and behavior toward that part of their personality.

After you are finished, draw a box around what you have written, and write at the top of the box, "Is this transference?"

At this point, don't be puzzled. Think about your family members. Are the personality characteristics of the person you wrote about and your reaction to it similar? Or is it a replay or re-creation of something that occurred in your relationship with one of your family members?

For example, are there familiar personality trait that causes you to react strongly? If so, perhaps this reaction is a transference from previous relationships.

Some may see the connection immediately, but some will not. To increase the power and complexity of the exercise, understand that transference may be trickier than simply reacting to others the way you reacted to one or both of your parents.

Use this section to write you own scenarios, we have listed some examples on the next page.

(if in training this is a perfect time to write on the board other scenarios)

•You notice the other in the same way you notice your parent when you were young (form of transference).

Examples

•You observe the other as being the way you wished your parent could have been (the idealized parent).

•You see the other as the child you were, and you behave like your parent did.

•You see the other as the child you were, and you behave like you wished your parent did.

With this added depth, it's easier to make the connection. There might not be any connection or may be unable to see it. It's okay.

EGO vs EGO

NOTES:

Organizational Changes

If you are like most people, anxiety ratchets up when you hear about organizational change. A few years ago, I read a book about a mouse and cheese. You may be familiar with the book. Like most who do not like change; Its uncomfortable and it can be stressful. However, change is unavoidable. As you read this, time is moving, and you are changing. You are learning something new. Isn't that change? Yes, it is great change. But what happens if the change is not as exciting as learning something new? Can there still be a learning curve? Absolutely!

Organizational change is just that – it's learning something new. How do you manage organizational change?

____
____
____
____
____
____

Reasons for change

Organizational change is necessary.
Companies often change with the times.
Retirements, customers, and products.

Time Management

If you are like most people, there are areas in your life that consumes your time and takes away your productivity. With emails, cell phones, trainings, and meetings, how can one person do it all? We have some tips for you. They are not set in stone. However, they are a great way to start managing your time. Good time management requires an important shift in focus, and this means going from "just doing" to "smashing" the outcome.

3 Steps to maximizing your time:

1. Prioritize

2. Set Goals

3. Focus

SMART Goal Template

Date:

Goal:

Is your goal SMART?

Specific: *What exactly will you accomplish? What are the requirements?*

What are the constraints?

Measurable: *How will you measure your progress? How will you know when you have reached this goal?*

Achievable: *How can the goal be accomplished? What are the logical steps you should take?*

Do you have the resources to achieve this goal? If not, how will you get them?

Relevant: *Why is this goal significant to your work? Is this goal in line with your long-term objectives?*

Timely: *When will you work on this goal? When is the completion of this goal due?*

THE EFFECTIVE PLANNER

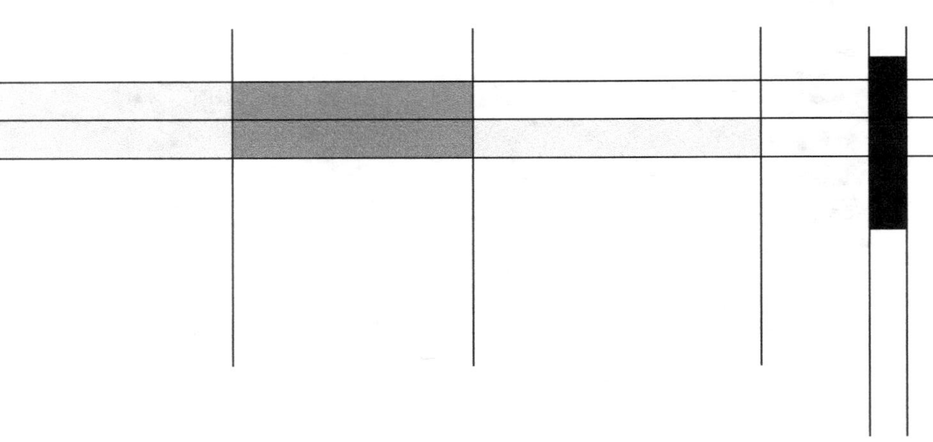

WEEKLY PLANNER

Date: _______________________

The Priorities:

1. _______________________
2. _______________________
3. _______________________
4. _______________________

To-Do:

- ◯ _______________________
- ◯ _______________________
- ◯ _______________________
- ◯ _______________________
- ◯ _______________________
- ◯ _______________________
- ◯ _______________________
- ◯ _______________________

Must Remember...

Events:

Monday

Tuesday

Wednesday

Thursday

Friday

Saturday

Sunday

My Weekly Mantra:

YOU are capable of *amazing* things

NOTES:

YOU *WIN!*

As Human Service Professional, you have made a tremendous mark on those in the communities you serve. It is my hope that you continue the work of developing skills that are needed in this ever-changing field of service.

If I could leave you with one more thought, it is to utilize the working relationships you have and process as much as possible to ward off burnout. Building a culture in your organization that is safe can help with the weight of responsibility that comes with the job.

Until we meet again, continue to do your best.

Stephanie Williams

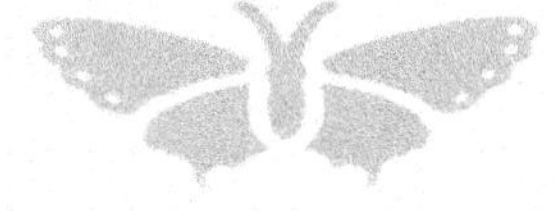